WOMAN INK

AI art by Niokoba © 2024
Cover design by Niokoba
Editorial services by H.L.R hlrwriter@outlook.com

All Rights Reserved
ISBN: 979-8-88913-221-9
First Edition

Published by Warren/Timothy Productions
Contact: https://timothytaylor-thepoet.com

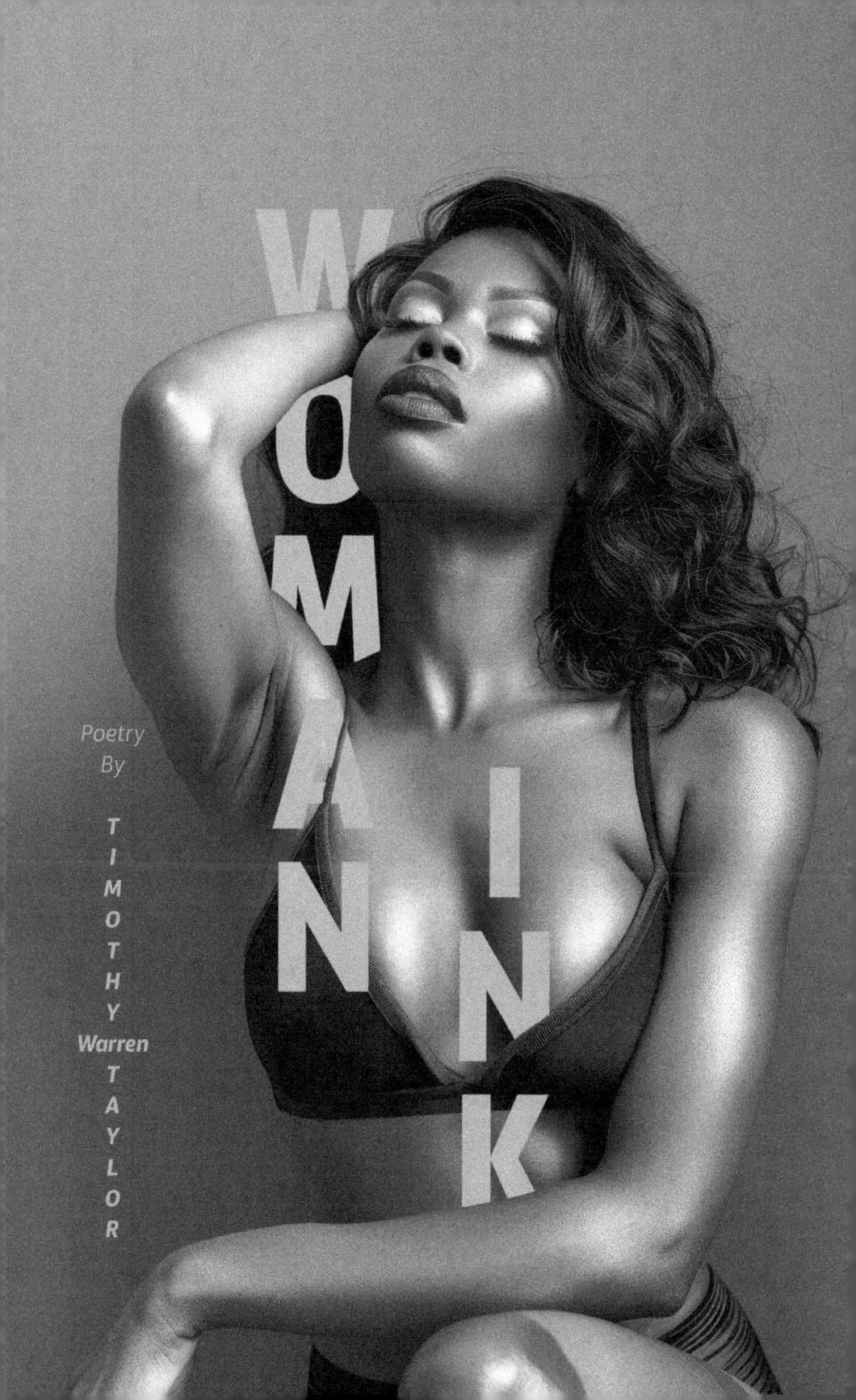

WOMAN INK

Poetry By

TIMOTHY

Warren

TAYLOR

CONTENTS

Chapter One
My Beginning

Chapter Two
Introvert/Extrovert

Chapter Three
My Evolution

Chapter Four
Muses

Woman **Ink**

DEDICATION

I dedicate this book to my lovely grandmothers, Willie Ray Person and Jessie May Taylor. Coming up as a kid, they truly were the kindest, beautiful, and most charismatic women I've ever met. They both had that southern charm and got along very well with each other. Jessie May passed away a few years ago, in her eighties. Willie Ray just turned ninety and is doing quite well. I love my mother, father, sister, son, nephews, aunts and uncles, but these two ladies were the only people in the world I could talk to about anything.

ACKNOWLEDGMENTS

I'd like to thank the Father, Son and Holy Spirit of Truth for blessing me with this incredible gift and the desire to manifest it into fruition. Sometimes I struggle with the sexual poems and wonder how much I should reveal, but I include them because I understand that sexuality is a part of the human condition and the poems are needed to paint a complete picture, to give the truest possible account of who I am and the times we are living in. Repetition is my gift to God and my understanding of how His creative process dwells in and around me at all times.

REPETITION (THE SECRET OF ALL)

Everything that is,
everything that does,
everything that will be,
everything that was
is through repetition.
The reason anything is possible,
the reason everything is possible
is because through repetition all things are.
Repetition is the reason why we reach out
for that distant star,
only to get there and realize
we haven't gone that far...

AUTHOR'S NOTE

Dear Readers,

I thought very long and hard about how to begin this book. In the end, I decided to make the introductory poem 'A Kiss and What Could Have Been'. In part, it was because the woman in that poem was the one who got away. But looking back on it now, she had just as much to do with shaping my heart as the rest of them.

So, ladies and gentlemen, I humbly present *Woman Ink*, in the hopes that you judge it in any way you deem fit.

A Kiss and What Could Have Been

Someday, when you're old and gray,
you may look back on this and miss me.
It may make you wonder what it was at the time
that made it so easy to dismiss me.

The angel I've been praying for
may have finally come along to assist me
and, for a moment in time, everything in your heart
may find it hard to resist me.

The what ifs or what could have been
may consume the depths of your heart immensely.
You may dream of my lips on yours
and feel the slow burn of their intensity.

The gravity of my love may become so deep
that you fall prey to its density
and finally see yourself through my eyes
and how long I've fantasized about you kissing me.

You may find yourself where I am right now,
remembering how you knew me way back when,
and spend the rest of the night questioning yourself
about a kiss and what could have been.

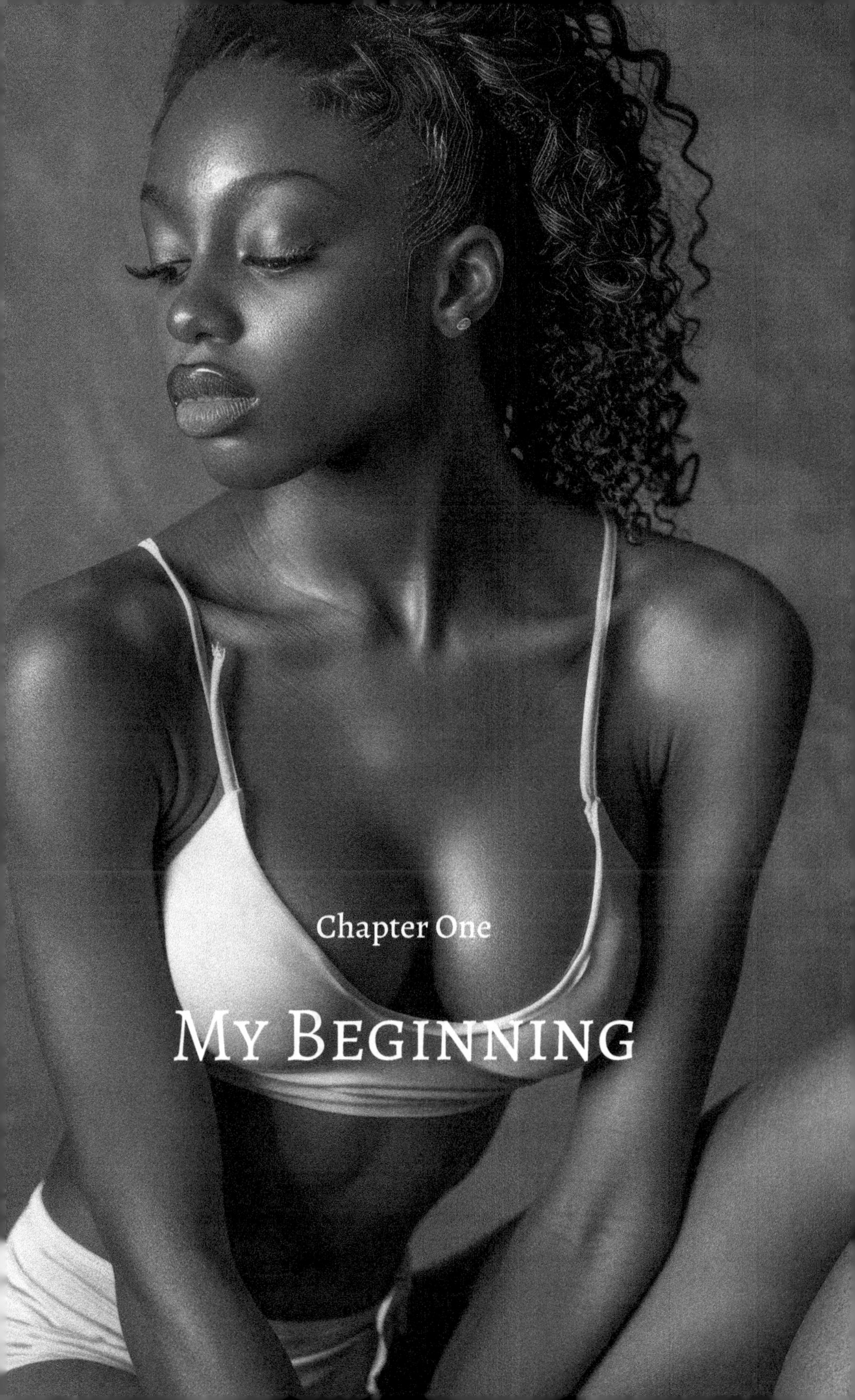

Chapter One

My Beginning

Throughout my entire childhood, I was extremely shy. I was an introvert who spent all my time after school in my room. On one particular day, I remember my mom and dad having an intense conversation in the dining room. They stopped as I entered. I returned to my room, and within minutes my mom knocked on my door before coming in. We sat on my bed, and she looked me right in the eyes and said, "Son, we love you, but we've been noticing that you don't go outside and play with the other kids. You're not into sports and you don't interact with girls. And, well, we were just wondering... are you gay?" Before I could answer in a flurry, she continued with, "If you are, it's okay. We love you. It doesn't matter." I chose to remain silent as she went on for about ten minutes, giving me the speech they had prepared, the one my father couldn't bear to be a part of.

When she finally gave me a chance to speak, my answer was, "No, I'm not gay, Mama." I think I was nine or ten when this conversation took place and it hurt me for reasons that I couldn't express. I couldn't explain that the shyness I felt didn't feel normal. I couldn't express that it felt like there was a spirit in me. The person I was felt trapped and subdued inside of me. And the ironic thing about it was that, at the time, I had a crush on two of my mother's closest friends. One was so pretty and petite, the other was gorgeous and had curves for days. I spent night after night wrestling with my erections, fantasizing about all the ways I wanted to have sex with them. There were so many evenings they came over, and I wanted to touch them in all the inappropriate places. And I was the only kid at the time so I got a lot of attention from both of them. There were so many times they would talk to me and we would all laugh and joke, but in the back of my mind the wheels were always turning. And I felt like they knew it. I felt like they were encouraging it because they thought it was cute. All I kept thinking to myself was, "Do I want this ass whooping today?" because in my little wet dreams I was wearing them out.

For sixteen years, I lived with a Soul Assassin.

SOUL ASSASSIN

He stood over me while I slept
and, as usual, didn't make a sound.
He remained as silent as the secrets he kept
whenever he left me bound,
bound by chains that remain
invisible to the naked eye,
that only ever glisten whenever
I'm left alone to ponder why,
why all the things I've wanted
from this existence never came to be.
I had no one else in the shadows
of this empty room to blame but me
for living my life night after night as a slave
to this shyness I feel within,
hoping I could find the strength to loosen his restraints
just enough to bend
the chains around this suppressed soul,
concealing who I really am,
and let one blessed moment make up for all the days
that I've felt damned.

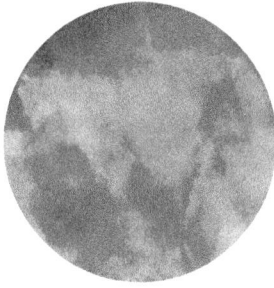

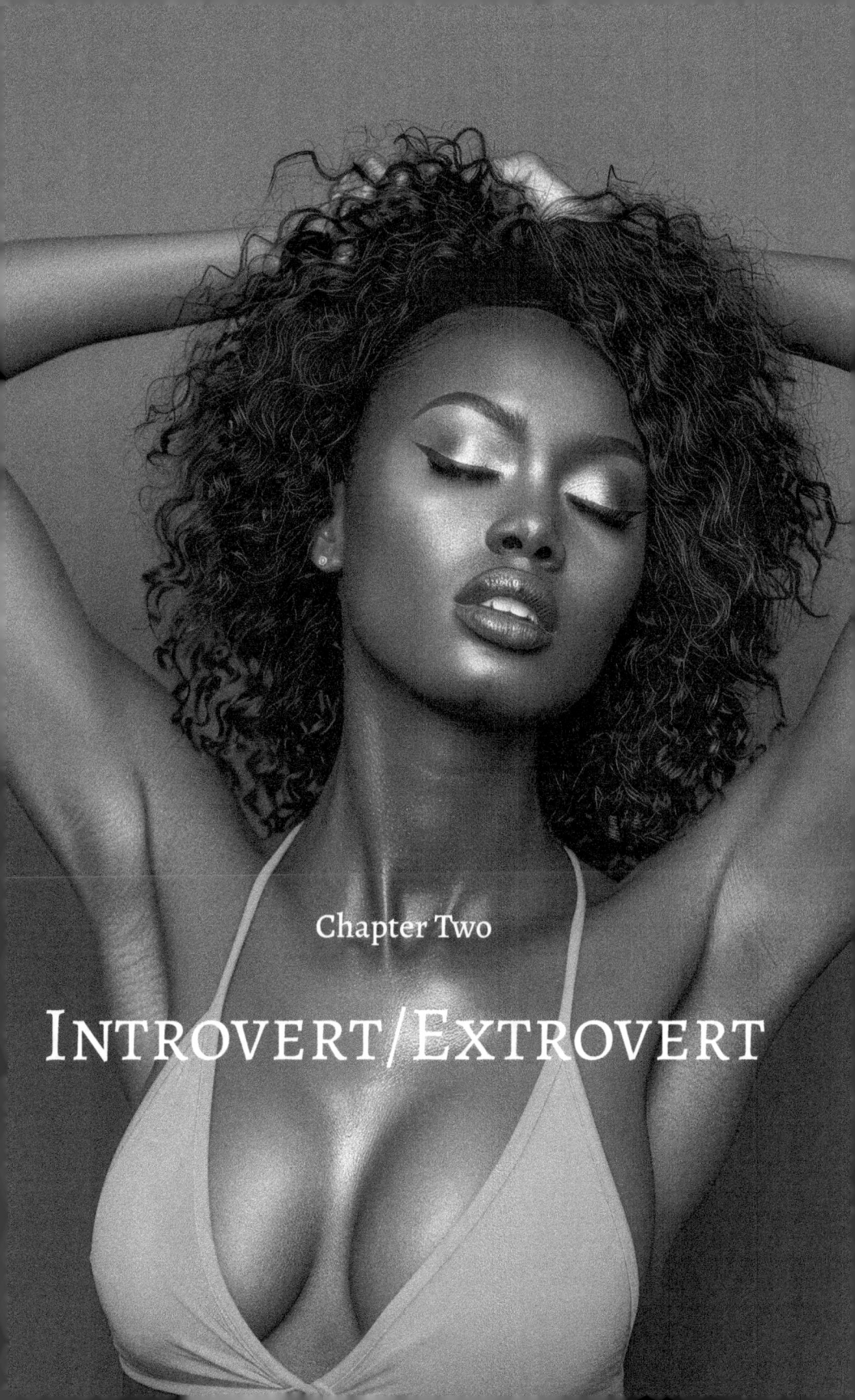

Chapter Two

Introvert/Extrovert

By the time I turned nineteen, I was an entirely different person. That three-year period of late adolescence astonished my parents because I had finally come into my own. I still had bouts of shyness but the extrovert in me was on ten. You see, the extrovert in me learned how to use that shyness to my advantage. A lot of older people called it "making up for a lost time". But back then I was too young to understand love and lust, and how what goes up must come down.

IF MY PENIS COULD TALK

If my penis could talk, he'd tell you
that eight inches always touched the bottom.
He'd say he's lived a fairytale, riding his Trojan
through silk linings on my bed of cotton.
He'd need a few languages to explain
all the ways he's given as good as he's gotten.
He'd have to thank Revlon and Maybelline
for all those shades that spoiled him rotten.

He'd say the quiet, fragile ones put in work —
never break and almost never fake.
He'd say the lazy ones talk too much shit,
lie there and say they'll do whatever it takes.
But the better of the two always managed
to find a way to make his veins pulsate
until the friction and the secretion stick like glue
and, in a day or two, chip away like snowflakes.

He'd say he used every soft smile and light sigh
to feed his ego like he always knew it.
He'd say, to tell the truth, he chose every dare
just to see if he could do it.
He'd swear the best lubricant in the universe
will always be a female's bodily fluids.
He'd thank his owner for all the nights he didn't rush
and wasn't afraid to put his back into it.

He'd say size doesn't matter because the best sex
comes from the dirty thoughts you think
and the most graceful art form will always be
the rhythm of two bodies in heat.
He'd compare pubic hair to furs
because they were always so plush, just like a mink.
He'd thank all those beautiful women who took the time
to make him feel so pretty in pink.

He'd say the great ones come over and over again,
like he had the power to fulfill a need.
The fast ones showed him how to shift gears
and satisfy a need for speed.
He'd say the slow, steady ones couldn't understand
the psychology behind his need to feed
because, at the time, out of the seven deadly sins
his favorite was always greed.

He'd speak of a charmed life
and how he's never known the fear of rejection.
He'd thank latex for all those nights in question
that he thought he needed protection.
He'd give glory to God
for the million and one things it took to make an erection.
He'd acknowledge everyone
that offered a helping hand in his desire to achieve perfection.

He'd say one was so sublime that when he was done
it was so much better than he thought
and that afterwards he'd have to help her down the steps
whenever she tried to walk.
He'd remind his owner (who just happens to be the author)
to think twice before he gets caught
because it takes big balls to write a poem called
'If My Penis Could Talk'.

SILVER SPOON
A letter to myself while drunk

Where are all those investors
when it seems you have nothing left to offer?
When it seems that there's nothing left to gain
that they can foster,
when your stock has finally crashed
and you've hit rock bottom,
and you find out that the only thing worse than death
is to be forgotten?

Where are all those incentives
they gave you when you were on your feet?
And all those sweet things they said about you
that made you feel unique?
Where's that guilt you felt all those times
you thought that you wronged them,
back when they were as submissive as little slaves
and behaved like you owned them?

Where are those tender ears, back when the sound
of your voice could turn their night into day?
Where are all those soft smiles when the world
was an oyster you had served your way?
Why do all the ones who told you
they'd love you till the end and through it all
only find the time to laugh at you with their new lovers
whenever you pick up the phone to call?

And why do all those brothers driving tricked-out cars,
with fresh clothes and new money,
drawing those pretty young mamas
like queen bees in search of honey,
knowing that once upon a time
they couldn't hold a candle to the style you had,
help you to understand
why anything with a broken wing must feel so sad?

Some say it's karma, what goes around
comes around and will always be,
while others believe it's the Holy Spirit of Truth
coming to set you free.
Others say, "If it doesn't kill you in the end,
it will only make you stronger,"
tempting you to rise out of the ashes
like a phoenix and feed upon your hunger.

But I believe it's not until you've lost everything
that you're free to do anything
and this is the part of the poem
where I give you a little taste of what I mean.
This is where I remind you that I'm leaving
the old you in this empty bottle of rum,
for how long I've planned to save
the best of who you are for the very next one
and watch you love her so hard for all the days

I've been down and had to live without,
till the old ones see y'all together
and wonder what that new you is about,
and watch the love of a good woman
uplift your self-esteem and reestablish my clout
while you feed her with the same silver spoon
I'm going to use to eat their hearts out.

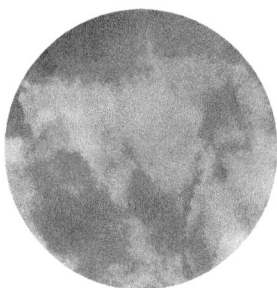

Chapter Three

MY EVOLUTION

'Silver Spoon' represents the moment the women all moved on. Some found boyfriends, some moved away and others went to college. That moment made me aware that time waits for no man. I came face to face with the fact that I had nothing to offer anyone except sex. I had no money, no job, and no car. The world had changed — they all moved on to something better and I got left behind. I didn't realize at that moment that sometimes something can hurt you so much that you mean what you're saying. From then on, I decided to get my life together and only pursue the kind of women I wanted, no matter the outcome.

METHODICAL
adj. in a systematic or orderly fashion

This is the portion of my heart that usually remains in the box,
where I keep all the rose petals that blossomed into love me not's
where I keep the emotions I never get to express
and the secrets that don't exist. I have yet to confess
my box full of words I never get to say —
from deep dark thoughts that never meet the light of day,
full of private moments that have yet to exist
and, for now, lack anyone to share them with.
Words that hide in the shadows of my daily façade
like stitches in the lining of a broken heart,
full of passion and tears that pour down untamed like the rain
over its lost love, to a time that never came.
This is the part of my heart that I almost never show
because of the knot and how tight I usually tie the bow,
where my innocence gives in to its nail-biting seductions
in the hopes of a love affair fraught with danger and the repercussions,
of unspeakable things that get done in the dark,
all waiting to be judged by our Lord and God
and be found guilty of feelings that, in reality, seem illogical,
that only have the desire to exist and become methodical.

LOST IN TRANSLATION

Whenever I say I want
someone who stimulates me intellectually,
it means I've never
really been comfortable with anyone sexually.
When I say an independent
woman is okay but I'd prefer a little dependency,
it means I've never been
with someone I could be myself with in an act of intimacy.
When I say I want someone
woman enough to be honest and keep it true,
I mean someone who doesn't feel
the need to lie or say anything she doesn't want to.
Whenever I say my turn-offs are
women who come across as superficial, phony or fake,
I mean I want someone I can
tickle during sex and laugh off the funny faces we make.
When I say I'm not
looking for someone to mistreat, misuse or make a fool of,
I really mean God could be
looking down on the only chance I get to find true love.
Whenever I say
I want someone I can trust long enough to drop my guard,
I mean I want a woman
whose pulse is the same rhythm as my own beating heart.

When I say I want someone
who will look into my eyes and see the goodness they reveal,
I mean I want a woman
who won't hurt me or make me ashamed of the way I feel.
Whenever I tell people
I want to grow old with someone who makes me feel young,
I really mean I want a woman
who's not afraid to climax sucking on my thumb.

But whenever I say I want to find her
standing somewhere in the sands of my imagination,
soaking wet from head to toe,
right out of the ocean of God's grand creation,
what I really mean
is so truly beautiful a thing, no words fit the summation
and all I have is a moment of silence
to describe how much gets lost in translation.

LOVE LETTER TO A DOLL MAKER

Body —
beautiful,
smile —
truthful,
wrapped in tender skin
with a broken heart to mend.
Eve's
blood,
Adam's
seed,
with a sexy mind
no eyes can read.
Thighs —
soft,
lips —
glossed,
with an ample body
so willing to feed
whatever,
wanting,
lust
or must,
from any dark desire
her man might need.

Pretty
little
eye
candy
that's sweeter than a now-or-later,
that proves my God is more than a God —
sometimes
he's a doll maker.

Note to readers: the apostrophes in 'Eve's blood' and 'Adam's seed' were adopted for structure. It was originally 'Eve is blood, Adam is seed', and both versions fit perfectly when read aloud.

THE LIE

Maybe I'm better off with nothing,
not even someone to have or hold,
when everyone who has something
seems to have sacrificed their soul.
Every day I go to work
I become another puppet on their strings;
I spend all my time trying to pay bills
until there's nothing left to chase my dreams.
Every time I have sex
I have to pretend to be someone else;
I wear the façade of a star-crossed lover
who, in truth, never learned to love himself.
And every day I grow older,
I seem to fail no matter how hard I try.
And every night I lay here and wonder,
"Is wisdom learning how to live within the lie?"

REDEMPTION

Can words tame this lust?
Are words ever enough
to describe the way I feel?
The phone rings and it's always a woman
in need of something —
offering her appeal,
stirring the seed deep within my soul
as I listen to her new story unfold
and the mysteries thereof,
hoping that this time
somehow the outcome will end in love
(even though, in the end, it never really does).

Because as she speaks: #&$%@!
my analytical mind starts to unravel the flaws
that always get washed away in the walls
between her milky thighs
and my mind goes to that place
where the heat of her tongue and little white lies
always end up as teardrops in her eyes.

And when the truth finally reveals itself
I have to stop and ask myself:
is happiness in the arms of someone else?
Or after a lifetime of heartache from countless tries,
can I learn to forgive the way this one cries
and let redemption for her be redemption for me
in our Father's eyes?

WHITE GIRL RIDER

Looking back,
I recall her being so fine
that before I could make my move
I had to literally
hold my breath and count to ten.

I remember exhaling
before saying something juvenile
like, "Guess what?"
and when she looked up,
Knight took Queen, so I went all in.

I told her how at first glance
there was a spiritual connection
because after one look in her eyes
it felt like I knew where heaven was at.

I asked her, if her heart was a book,
which page would describe
how much desire I'd taste
in that first awkward kiss if our lips ever met.

She smiled and said that by the way,
I was undressing her with my eyes.
Feeding off my vibe, didn't take a psychic
to let her know where my head was at.

So we laughed before we discussed
the proverbial elephant in the room,
only to find out
we were both comfortable in our own skins.
Now, can you imagine that?

So I leaned into it and asked her
would our first time be a slave fantasy
or could the schoolgirl in her get off
role-playing as a teacher's pet?

The back and forth felt whimsical,
like a seductive little dance,
where I marveled at how well her foxtrot
kept up with my nickel slick quick-step.

I remember my stomach growling
so I decided to use it when I told her
something about the way she looked
reminded me that I hadn't eaten yet.
I asked her to tell me more about herself
because I had been trying to figure out
what kind of London dove or Salem witch
made her so soft and wet.

*

Anyway, I knew I had her when
I asked her to meet me at the spot
and I heard her voice tremble a little
moments before she asked me, "Where?"

I gave her the location of a house party
that just happened to be on later that night
and told her I would love it if she could come
and how I would meet her there.

I told her if I couldn't pick her up
and transportation was a problem,
just catch a cab and I'd be all too happy
to come out and pay the fare.

I told her it was the house on the corner
so if she got lost all she had to do
was follow the scent of cocoa butter
and all that Black girl magic in the air.
She asked why her
and I remember thinking because
she was wrapped in a kinda package
my hands wanted to handle with so much care.

She gave me heavy eye contact,
so I flipped it on her
when I told her I wanted to spend all night slow
dancing with that curiosity behind her stare.

I had never seen anything like her before;
she was truly one of a kind.
It felt like the suburbs finally gave the inner city
something beautiful that we could share.

Our first kiss was on the dancefloor
and she made it feel like the Fourth of July,
Mardi Gras, carnival in Brazil
and a day at the World's Fair.

*

Now over time she changed the way she talked.
The neighborhood changed the way she walked
and her demeanor adopted a hint
of Black girl swagger in her style.
Everybody loved her —
she was finally one of us.
She started sporting French braids
and the whole thing drove her mother wild.

After a few months of foreplay, she asked,
"How do I know you're not color-struck
and looking for a white girl
with a nice shape
who just might be a pretty good dick rider?"

So I hit her with the Spielberg
(before I even knew it was Spielberg's)
when I told her it's not about color
if I get to play with the avatar inside her.

So she hit me back with a fantasy
of showing up at my doorstep
in her favorite pair of tight jeans
and a Little Red riding hood.

She said she finally felt comfortable
and was ready to climb the oak tree
if I promised to leave her cherry soaking wet
all over my morning wood.

But on the night before, while we were on the phone,
they got into an argument
she told her mother everything
and, at the time, I didn't know what to say.

I didn't hear from her for about a week
and when I finally went by
it broke my heart when the neighbors told me
that they had moved away.

THE MORAL OF THE STORY OF 'WHITE GIRL RIDER'

So here's the moral of the story...

When you're young, you think you can change the world. So, young people, change it! Do it for all us kids who couldn't. Live how you wanna live, love who you wanna love, and do what you wanna do. You didn't make this racist system, but you and you alone have the power to change it.

And in case you're wondering what ever happened to the girl in the poem, I did too for a very long time, and it hurt my soul to hear she got married to a man who abused her, was in and out of jail and left her with a house full of little ones. You know, the one her mother chose.

And me, well, my life got better and better every year. Because I started from the bottom and now I'm here...

THE ONE & ONLY

I've been the main,

I've been the side,

but I've never been the one and only.

I've been happy,

I've been sad,

both emotions left me lonely.

I've had voluptuous,

I've had petite,

but I've never had what some call bony.

I've had smiles,

I've had frowns,

that in retrospect revealed were phony.

I've been patient,

I've rushed in,

and been myself in the time it took to know me.

I've had victims,

I've had villains,

both use sex in the times it took to show me.

I've had deceit

and mind games

played in their bitter attempts to turn me.

I've had lies

and fake tears

that were meant to steal my joy and burn me.

I've had ups,
I've had downs,
hoping to find her at the end of my journey.
I've been blessed,
I've been a curse,
but I've never been the one and only.

Chapter Four

Muses

I've given wings to this gift God saw fit to bestow upon me from the very first feather because somewhere in the mix I felt the lift and knew she was made to fly in all weather...

There were times I gave up on this gift but it didn't give up on me. There were times this gift gave up on me but I didn't give up on it. And now all I pray is that this book never goes out of circulation...

MONTEGO...

Pride:
come eat off my fork
and let my spoon feed your ego.
Lust:
come drink out my cup
until my thirst quenches your libido.
Sex:
come climax
until our one plus one equals
multiples
that make the prequel
almost as good as all our sequels.
Love:
come experience
blushes so rare they leave you feeling regal.
Temptations:
come experience
thoughts so bare we barely call them legal.
Euphoria:
wrap me in your super fly
and take me high just like an eagle.
Bliss:
hold on while I kiss the sky until
my Hendrix feels as fab as a Beatle.

Karma:

come reap what you sow

and don't be afraid to thread your needle.

Fate:

come roll your dice.

I want to risk it all in your casino.

Patience:

come unwind and spend time

like a hand on my amigo.

Destiny:

bring me a honey, lover, friend

to be my bae like Montego.

THE SURFACE

From the first time I saw her, I wanted to let her in,
into this flesh and blood that beats in a lion's den,
that's alive in a love that angels make
but still fragile enough for a woman's touch to break,
that leaves me in a constant pursuit of something more,
that's deeper and sweeter than anything I've had before,
until I wonder: does anyone really know the heart of mice and men?
When the thought of losing her would probably make me regret the win
so I string her along with the same casual conversations I use as bait
that keeps my relationships light as a feather when I measure their weight
until she never feels the center of my soul's warm core
or gets to see the nesting place in my heart where eagles soar.
Because nowadays I think twice before I let something beautiful begin
because of how complicated the maze gets before I reach the end
so all those deep feelings I'm supposed to feel I often fake
when I reach the breaking point of what my heart can take,
because I can't play in her black sands or swim in her warm shore
and when it's all said and done, watch her leave me wanting more.
That is, until I learn to trust in all the things I really want to see
from a woman who'll allow me to be as deep in love as I want to be.
And she'd have to be someone willing to give that same deep love back
before I show her that side of me that rivals Cyrano de Bergerac,
because I can't begin to tell her all the ways she'd give this love purpose
or about the heaven in my heart awaiting her underneath its surface.

ECSTASY FROM AN INNOCENCE LOST

Sexy was:

      all those passion marks

      she let me put on her neck;

      the frenzy of sounds

      she made that I didn't expect;

      that good girl image

      she was always trying to protect;

      whenever she told me

      all she wanted was my respect.

Sexy was:

      how she made each day

      feel like she just met me;

      how badly we wanted to have sex

      but she wouldn't let me;

      how it was never yes or no

      and I was alright with maybe

      because deep down inside

      I wanted her to have my baby.

Sexy was:

      how her slightest touch

      made my temperature rise;

      watching the sunset

      in those hazel brown eyes;

      the way she fed me;

      the flutter of her butterflies,

      how they electrified

      every time I touched her thighs.

Sexy was:

       the grown-up way

       she used to keep her legs crossed;

       the way she finally let me kiss

       all that lip gloss off;

       whatever made her tongue wet

       and her lips so soft;

       and all the ecstasy we experienced

       from an innocence lost.

STARS

Sometimes the flames of this love get so high
I fear they might burn me
and Cupid feels like the slave I set free
who now seems to own me
because he's got me doing things
I once laughed about
and thinking someone I didn't know before
is someone I can't live without.
As he pierces me with the brazen arrow of his almighty bow
until I'm caught up in the spells he cast to make the oceans flow
like all the while my heart is a prison he's been secretly guarding
that's got me doing life with no chance of parole or a plea bargain,
as a member of the chain gang plowing the fields of his rose garden
for another offering of rose petals to lay at her tender feet
and another chance to hang on all those soft words she speaks,
hoping she'll seduce me with a kiss that would leave Eden burning
and leave my head spinning on the axis that keeps the whole world turning.
As I walk the yard, daydreaming of my great escape.
Being forced to leave our next encounter up to fate
while chained up in the rings of my solitary confinement,
looking out the bars at how the stars and moon are all in alignment.
In this labor of love that puts the sun on my face all day
and makes Cupid crack his whip whenever I lose my way
until my fingers bleed from thorns and my back burns from scars:
and is the reason why I look in her eyes and all I see are stars...

DEEPER STILL

You are Beauty to the Beast,
my own nasty little piece of perfect passion candy.
You're my secret untold,
the key to my soul unlocking all it can be.

You're my number one stunner,
my long hot summer of sex on the beach.
You're the smile on my face
as I lick, suck and taste the circumference of your peach.

Baby, you're my deeper still,
my Miss "I missed the pill" and it's yours for the making.
You're my "Baby, stop,
before I call the cops" 'because it's ripe for the taking.

Baby, you're my "so hot
I just can't stop this waterfall flowing within".
You're my "in the beginning",
my apple bitten, and the reason that I sin.

THIS EMPTY SOUL OF MINE

Yes, this wasn't much of a life before her touch.
And I guess I'm guilty of loving her way too much
because just when I thought life couldn't be better,
she left me alone to face forever.

And now all of a sudden, heaven seems out of reach.
Even when I hear my pastor preach
it feels like I've followed the rainbow to my pot of gold
only to find, inside, my own empty soul.

Because my genie in her bottle
has gone off and left the bottle hollow.
She's run off to a place that I cannot follow
without leaving my broken heart behind.

And it feels like the sun won't shine on tomorrow,
like I'm drowning in a pool of my own sorrow
and God has no love left that I can borrow
without leaving Him, this empty soul of mine.

KRYPTONITE

How do I turn a one-time event into something we do every night?
And make it our time spent giving it to you just the way you like?
Where I become that Mister Lover Man, bent on doing you right
until you think the taste of Tim was meant to feed your appetite?

You know, that dark man of mystery intent on becoming your type,
the one in your dreams, your fantasies lent to live up to all the hype,
that good thing heaven sent to bask in the afterglow of your magnificent light
for the only daughter of Eve with the scent of a woman, he found ripe.

That someone with something on the rent to role-play in your crib to-nite,
pay the price of admission to hear you vent passion all over his open mic
and be the chocolate covered mint on the bed of feathers he uses to take flight
and spend every cent for the elution he's licking and sucking on his Mrs. Right.

The tongue twister you leave pent, waiting to break the skin on that first bite
of the apple of his eye that he became content with at first sight,
who leaves him shy like Clark Kent whenever he thinks about holding you tight,
hoping the 'S' on his chest is a hint you could be that kryptonite.

BUTTERFLIES & UNICORNS

Butterflies flutter as she stands there naked,
soaking wet in nothing but soap suds.
Unicorns rise as I admire the tapestry
of a sex appeal blooming like rosebuds.

There's a hint of jasmine still lingering in the air
from the steam and acrylic in her backdrop
that always manages to make her nasty.
So clean I just want to beat until my heart stops.

Butterflies spiral as I look down, staring
at that Pretty Young Thing below her waist.
Unicorns fly and my heart skips a beat
from the expression Nefertiti puts on her face.

And I start to ponder which I love more
in the contest between her nipples and her dimples
until those thoughts fade from the sexy way
she uses that beautiful thing between her temples.

Butterflies tease me throughout our foreplay
as I slowly rise, waiting to feel her grip.
Unicorns nod as I feel their throb
from the adrenaline waiting for her on my tip.

So I let her do her thing and reinvent herself
with her ability to make all things new
because I know it's good, I've been here before.
She made our first time feel like déjà vu.

Only erotic butterflies designed by God
could make curves on a frame so slender, this sleek.
We don't talk much; we have nothing in common
so we let our mouths moan until our emotions speak.

Unicorns got me denying my flesh
and starving myself to achieve the lust I seek.
They've got me practicing abstinence in silence
so I can leave her on her tippy-toes when I peak.

"This could end at any time; all we have is now"
is the mantra she allows to become her myopia
because she knows it makes me come alive
and feel as wild as Africa in her utopia.

So I fully intend to make my impression felt
until I burn out and she goes supernova
because if I don't get forever, that's alright,
as long as I make her miss me when it's over.

6/9 SECONDS IN THE LIFE OF AN ICE CREAM CONE

Lips juicy,

skin soft,

flesh of spiritual silk.

Saliva wet,

liquid sugar

&

breast of natural milk.

Hair long,

raven black,

tongue fat & thick.

Sexy neck,

nefarious heart

&

a mind nickel slick.

Oval mouth,

pink lip gloss,

I make whip cream white.

Hot breath,

deep throat

&

clean teeth I find so polite.

Slowly
swallowing
every drop of freedom that I leak,
all with a delicious smile
&
the rhythm of a dancer when I peak.

Blowing my mind with the sexy way
she always makes the glitter shine,
that on a scale from one to ten
always gives my first six her best nine.

THE REOCCURRING ONE-NIGHT STAND

Her body is drenched.
My thirst is quenched.
We finally fed the hunger.
She has no strength to speak.
Her body is asleep
from the spell lust put us under.

I lie awake because I can't surrender.
I can't stay the night because I still remember
how much I'd rather be alone.
I remember all the games I had to play
and all the things I had to say
in those moments of weakness that came and left me strong.

I remember wiping away the tears she'd cry,
listening to all her reasons why
and pretending to believe every lie she tells to draw me near.
And how the only times it seems worth its while,
the only times I ever really mean my smile,
is when she does whatever it takes to keep me here.

And I get to work out my frustrations all night long,
usually humming the words to some sad love song,
wondering does my discontentment ever show
from how often I've let her bullshit faze me
or how the moment this relationship felt like slavery
became money by her bed for the freedom to come and go.

My friends ask me why I stay.
Why do I continue to live my life this way
with someone whose only purpose seems to be to keep me bound?
But I always let my ego choose what I say
when I tell them that the question I ask myself every day is:
why do the crazy ones always give the best head in town?

But what if I told you it's deeper than that?
What if I told you there's a matter of fact
I need to overcome but I don't know if I can?
What if I told you it's a spiritual hold?
She has a tie on my soul and with her I come
face to face with the dark side of who I am.

She understands the psychology of my heart
and everything she does in the light or the dark
gives me great joy or great sorrow at her command.
She enjoys bringing out the worst in me
and allows me to be as bad as I want to be,
just to wash away any delusions I have of being a good man.

Because she knows that sexy shit she puts on my mind
and all those fantasies she leaves behind
makes the thought of another woman feel so bland.
She knows when to say what I want to hear
and she knows that the only thing I fear
is the thought of her walking away holding another hand.

What if I told you that, fast or slow,
she devours my libido
with a grip she keeps tighter than a rubber band?
I hate saying yes but I can't say *no*,
I want to leave but I can't let go
because I'm so addicted to her--- supply and her demand.

What if I told you I secretly fault myself
because I'm too mature to blame her or anyone else
for being a fool who keeps trying to build his foundation in her sand?
Or that she's playing me right, no matter how much I trip,
because she knows I only get off on relationships
with women who should have always only ever been a one-night stand?

THIRSTY

She's always a liar.
The truth too often stands in front of what she desires
and oftentimes her downfall
has muscles, brown skin, and stands at least six-feet tall.

She's never satisfied with what she has
because to her the future is in a race with her past
and whatever feeds her ego becomes the crutch
she uses to disrespect any man who doesn't have as much.

She will always be the one who contradiction loves
because whatever she says she won't do, she eventually does.
And whenever she falls in love and gives her heart to a man
he's usually the dirtiest piece of mud God ever made from sand.

Because she derives all her pleasure from her pain
so while other women admire Abel, she secretly desires Cain.
But she has a sweet, seductive side
she shows then she hides that's meant to leave her lover deprived
until he spends all his time going through the ups and downs
of all the joys and sorrows her heart prescribes.
And he damn near loses his mind before the end
until she decides to show him that sweet, seductive side again.

But y'all, I love this woman so damn deeply
that at times it feels like the Lord has cursed me
because if I had to choose between this Black woman or water,
my well could overflow but I'd die here, thirsty.

ECLIPSE

My heart feels so heavy on the dark side of its seclusion.
Outside there's a full moon casting light from its lunar intrusion.
Inside, my heart aches from another heartbreak
and in the dark of night while the world is asleep, I lie here awake,
restless in my despair.

And the moon looks so heavy hanging there,
suspended on invisible strings in mid-air,
watching me come back to the same conclusion
that maybe the happiness I seek is all an illusion.

And its cold, pale face becomes the light it lends
to help solidify this cold, lonely place I feel within.
Filling the empty void I feel in my heart's desolation,
making this room as cold as the North Pole the moment love went on vacation.

And as the moonlight shines through the window onto her pillowcase,
baring the same light that once shined down on her sleeping face,
it feels like I'm on the dark side of the moon in total isolation,
lying here by the phone, all alone with my righteous indignation.

And it's not that I can't forgive. I forgive — not to would be a sin.
It's just that once some things are done, they can never be undone again.
And this same lunar moon that makes the tides roar from its effect
is behind the heaviness in my heart and is deepening its neglect.

Because I know if she were here tonight, we'd be making love.
And before I fall asleep, those memories will be what I think of
as I close my eyes, remembering how I used to suck on her pretty lips,
and hoping tomorrow when I wake up there won't be an eclipse.

'M'

Many years ago my grandmother decided to play matchmaker and set me up with one of her best friend's daughters. So we talked on the phone for a few weeks and eventually I went to the mall to meet her. I brought her roses and I remember her being so hard to get that I promised to take her to Vegas as an official first date. Of course she didn't believe me, but after a few months of unofficial dinners and movies, she invited me back to her place. When she called me, she told me the door would be unlocked and that I should let myself in. When I showed up, she came out of her bathroom covered in nothing but soap suds.

She had pretty eyes, long legs and incredible thighs. But the thing that really got me was it was the first time I had ever seen silver dollar nipples on big, beautiful, canary yellow breasts. So we took it to the bedroom. But once inside, she was so bold, nothing happened because I couldn't get it up. I was used to passive women who gave me complete control. So needless to say she began to talk about my ass to my face for about thirty minutes until I got dressed and left. I can still hear her now. "Oh, you told me I was going see stars, you said I was gonna cum all night, you told me you had that big dick, I guess you meant that limp dick and now you wanna get dressed and leave, huh? Lock my door, nigga." And as I closed the door she screamed out, "You limp dick bastard!"

The next day I told my grandmother what happened, and she and my grandfather laughed for hours. My grandmother told me, "Don't you know she's just messing with your head? Ignore her and get back over there and show her who you really are." And there goes my grandfather, "Yeah, limp dick bastard, go on back down there and get yo ass cussed out again." I love them — Mississippi grandparents are the best!

I was pleasantly surprised that it only took one call to get a second chance. So when I got there, I took my grandmother's advice and I ignored all the negativity that came out of her mouth just long enough to wear her ass out. And in the pandemonium of all her biting, scratching and clawing, it happened: we came. We came with her sucking on my thumb and me licking the oval shape of her sexy lips as they wrapped around it.

A couple of days later I went back to my grandma's to wash some clothes and when I took my shirt off she said, "What the hell is that girl doing to you?" I had hickeys, scratches and bite marks that broke the skin. She said, "How on earth did she put that hickey on the back of your neck!?"

My grandma was in disbelief and all I could do was laugh.

Having sex with 'M' was like performing an exorcism. And after that night and from that moment on, she always called me Mr. Taylor in the bedroom. 'M' gave me three years of unbelievable sex, full of rich, deep, animalistic moans that always ended in, "OH! OH! Mr. Taylor, you wearing this pussy out!!!" And oh yeah, by the way, just in case you were wondering, Vegas was incredible.

We reached out to each other last year for a little reunion sex and after all these years it amazes me that she can still push my buttons.

I CALL THIS ONE "FOREPLAY"

Sunday, January 1, 2017

Happy New Year handsome.
I'm just waking up
5:38 AM

Happy New Year. What's on
your agenda today
2:17 PM

Hanging out with the family in
Michigan city
3:17 PM

Friday, January 6, 2017

8:46 AM   Good morning sweetheart

Good Mr. Taylor   10:44 AM

Good morning Mr. Taylor   10:45 AM

Sunday, January 8, 2017

Hey what you doing   6:07 PM

Hey sweetheart I was out
when you texted. I am
getting ready for work in the
11:00 PM   morning.

Tuesday, January 17, 2017

Good morning sweetheart
how are you?
9:38 AM

Gm. I'm good. I was just thinking about yesterday. I was like Tim must have a woman now I haven't heard from him and I called u one day no repond
9:40 AM

Really, I wasn't aware of your call. I've been going out a lot lately but no woman yet. Lol
9:42 AM

Good luck. I'm engaged 11:32 AM

11:47 AM Congrats

So you mean I was taking you out and inviting you over and you had a nigga and was in a serious relationship. Wow!!! Congratulations anyway though and good luck to yall.
11:58 AM

I thought it was a friendly invite. What I owe you? By the way you got to MANY hang ups. I want you to be properly introduced to him. He no who u r

12:19 PM

Lol. Nall you alright, enjoy married life.

12:21 PM

Oh yeah and before I forget, you know fucking well I wouldn't have been taking you out or inviting you over if I knew you had a man. But I can't trip because apparently those games work for you, after all you're winning.

12:32 PM

Y not? It's only food. And I wasn't a pest becuz I only came by a couple of times

12:59 PM

He's not from the internet

1:05 PM

A very wise woman once told me that I'm somebody in my eyes if I'm nobody in yours. Take it easy.

1:06 PM

U always try to be sneaky but game recognizes game. Have all the internet goes u want. Just be careful becuz I care for you as a friend

That will be me   1:07 PM

I'm not needy. Remember u said I like needy women and they get usage out of u then they kiss u bye.   1:10 PM

So fucking what I'm online. I'm on a couple of sites. That doesn't mean I have a woman. And that ain't none of your damn business. Your business is marrying your fucking boo. My business is getting on with my life. So in short, fuck your wedding, fuck your groom, fuck your bridesmaids, fuck the best man, fuck the pastor, choir and flower girl, fuck your guest and there gifts, fuck your fake ass happily ever after bullshit. And in case I've forgot anyone, I'm a little tired...   1:16 PM

Lol. Wow !!! We still love you boo

1:17 PM

Keep playing with me and I WILL SHOW UP AND SHOW THE FUCK OUT!!!

1:19 PM

Hey for real what's your address so I can send u a invitation for u and all your internet boos just pick one don't matter

Please.

Please show up. He wants to properly introduce to u. He already knows I went out to dinner with

1:29 PM

I will send it to your granny house. I no her address

We will be at home at 6

1:55 PM

Good morning. First of all I would like to apologize for my behavior the other day. I just was having a bad day. I'm not engaged. I just said that to see how you feel becuz I felt you had been ignoring me. We have known each other to long to be playing games with each other. All I ask for is respect and I give it back in return. But you didn't have to say fuck the flower girl and the pastor. I was like damn .lol

9:30 AM

OUTSIDE MY/SELF:
TO MY COUSIN'S EX-GIRLFRIEND

If I stepped outside myself...
hmm... here I go.

Baby,
my M.J
wouldn't stop
until you get enough.

You'd go hard
in the paint
every time I let
you stroke the brush.

I'd be a phantom
in your opera
and steal your breath
with every rush.

Sweetheart,
I'd be a
Zodiac killer
every time I lick the cusp.

I promise
you'll be twisting,
turning, moaning
and doing the most.

My Harvey Wallbanger
will make you
leave scratches
on the post.

Come spend a night
in this supernatural
and if you need a guide
I'll be your host

because this
out-of-body experience
won't end
till I'm licking on your ghost.

If I stepped
outside myself,
I'd make you shake
until you shiver.

I'd lick on that piñata
till
my beard glistens
with your glitter.

I'll have you
chasing waterfalls
off this middle finger's
come hither.

Sugar,
I make sex shooters
every time
I squeeze the trigger.

You'd be devoured
in repetitions
of lick, suck,
swallow and repeat

until the algorithms
make
every sentence you speak
incomplete.
I'd spit fire
till your
pretty little squirts
turn into a skeet.

Lakema,
who in the hell
ever told you
that a Black goat can't eat???

If I stepped outside myself
and was no longer
that person
you knew before,

my
Adam's apple
wouldn't rest
till I got to taste your core.

You'd catch
multiples
in the symmetry
of this double metaphor.
Because little Dorothy
I promise you
you won't be
in Kansas anymore.

I'd take my time
with this fat tongue
until you
enjoy every lick,

make you cum
all in cursive
off my mentals
nickel slick.

Lick you
till my blunt
gives a contact
off every hit.

Make you cream,
thick like milk,
every time I taste
your quick.

Because you remind me
of that sitter
who taught me
how to make a dime shine
before hood chicks
like Thelma
made me enjoy it
like good times.

You're in this poem
because I think
you're as sexy
as the rhythm of my rhymes,

but sweetheart
you won't be a bad
bitch
until I see your canines.

(H.L.F.Y) x 2

I came home early from work today.
The house was dark and empty.
Her perfume is in the air
and there's a cigar still lit
by two glasses of champagne in the living room.
There's a trail of clothing leading down the hall
and her panties are in front of the door
that leads to our bedroom.
I hear her moans through the door,
a man cursing and our bed squeaking.
as I enter to the sounds of our TV
playing a video of our honeymoon
and a note on the bed that simply read:

    Happy Anniversary.
    I heard you were coming home early
    but I had to leave in a hurry
    to take the kids to the zoo.

So whatever you felt or thought before you opened that door,
Just remember the girl in the video
and multiply (Her. Love. For. You) x 2.

MODERN-DAY LOVE LETTER

I really want some dick!!

Lol... by the time I finish up you'll be out the mood

That dick was too good. It's something about when the dick is real good I crave for it more

All I've been thinking about today was you telling me you want some doggy style and fucking my shit up....

TIGHT

As I rest my head
on the small of her back
and admire the arch of her incline,
letting my fingers play
in the saliva, still wet,
and running down her spine

I can feel her fall asleep
as I stare
at my DNA all over her, from behind,
as I patiently wait
to press play
and masturbate to our rewind.

Before, during, and after
sex
I can feel her heartbeat race.
Her deep sleep
from the snatch and grab
lets me know she enjoyed the chase.

Usually, I press pause
to study
the expressions on her face
but tonight was special —
we've got whip cream
all over the walls, windows and a pillow case.

Who knew
such a pretty little thing
could ever be so much fun?
The way she kisses the head
and licks the tip
always makes me feel so young.

She makes all four seasons
feel like spring
so guess what? I think I'm sprung.
Because in this life
all I want is her
world without end until our kingdoms come.

She takes pride
in giving it to me whenever I want it,
just the way I like.
She believes in patience
so she takes her time
even if it takes all night.

I've never won an argument
but that's okay, I'm content
with being wrong even when I'm right,
because I wouldn't want a moment of anger
to take away any of that pride
she uses to keep it tight.

I Bear Alone

How do I describe what's in my heart
for someone who doesn't want to be?
Who, out of all the people she's ever known,
would rather it least of all be me.

Someone who, no matter how hard she tried,
could never bring herself to love me
and at times found all the beauty in my heart
to be the thing she found so ugly.

How do I explain how often I've wondered
how she was or prayed she was alright,
hoping she was happy or even in love,
in spite of what I go through every night?

How do I tell her she's still the only one
to this day that I'd die for?
And even as I write, I'm not ashamed to admit
that at times it's her I still cry for.

How do I say this is me apologizing
for these clumsy hands if they ever held her wrong?
Or the way I feel will always be me, hoping
this heavy burden that I carry, I bear alone.

ABOUT LAST NIGHT

Have you ever tasted something so good
you had to fight the temptation to bite?
And in the struggle, for lack of a better word
all you could do was call it 'tight'?

Have you ever had a twisted fantasy, and a dark dream
converge into something so right
that it forces you to spend all morning thinking
about last night?

I'm talking about revenge sex that was so good
I can still taste the spite —
from a cold-blooded lust that required my passion
to cool its winter white,

with flashes of brilliance in need of forgiveness
that still forces this hand to write,
asking if you, the reader, have ever spent all morning
thinking about last night.

I'm talking about an old flame rekindled
by hot wax and candlelight,
from a chance event, absent of emotions, that
might have made us feel contrite.

She came with no delusions of how the night
would end after their bitter fight —
just a sad story with a plot in need of my
character to change her plight.

I'm talking dimples, brown skin
and all the amenities I like;
equipped with ample hips, soft lips
and teeth I found so polite.

Who knew turning a frown upside down could
create a smile so bright?
So I'll ask again, have you ever spent all morning
thinking about last night?

DEVOURED

Seduction is an art form, you see...
All I need is one conversation under an exit sign
to plant my seeds and leave them watering in your head
until those thoughts become so scarlet
that the fire in your heart can't wait to paint them red,

followed by all those nights of insomnia you spend
thinking about whatever it was I said
until those seeds grow into the most beautiful garden
and become rose petals by our bed.

Now fast forward to a few months later when you're attached
because of all the ways you keep on choosing me
and I start to recognize all those false faces
you use in your feeble attempts to confuse me.

Because you're addicted to the cream you get
from all the ways your body keeps on using me
and that fear in your pit has turned into a phobia
that keeps entertaining the thought of someday losing me.

Because I've tapped into that primal part of you
that's so savage it makes the rest feel like a coward,
the one subdued by all those nasty fantasies
you've had too hot, too cold, or golden showered,

you know that inner freak you've been keeping on a leash
for fear of her someday being empowered
who, if she could, would unlock the door right now,
spread your legs and wait to be devoured...

ETERNITY

It's in her eyes,
the slender length of her neck,
the arch of her back,
that smile I can't forget.

The admiration I feel
looking at my creator's work,
thanking Him for the thousand
and one things that make her so dope,

that in my day-to-day struggles
give me the ability to cope
and in my darkest hours
fill my heart with hope.

As I lie here in the quiet
before our next storm,
holding her in my arms,
admiring the symmetry of her poem,

watching her sleep,
feasting off this food from a God
that comes from hearing the beat
and knowing I'm in her heart.

And if the truth be told,
then allow me to keep it honest:
yesterday is gone forever
and tomorrow is not promised,

but wondering if we'll make it
and praying we do somehow
has taught me to appreciate the moment
and live in the here and now.

We argued earlier
but that's okay —
God knew all it took to change my mind
was to change my view.

She asked me
why I wanted this forever
and I told her it's because I understand eternity
looking at you.

SUBMISSIVE

I turned to her as if to ask,
"Do you feel that?"
wondering if she could hear me
and after a short pause and her
trying to read my mind,
I replied, "Baby, that's chemistry..."

I told her
I can feel the elixir stirring
that's been waiting
and hoping she was into me
finally swirling around
and about to pour down
on how good tonight is finna be.

Because every step taken
lead us here and we both know
how much we've been wanting it.
So whatever happens next
was meant to be
and just waiting to come alive in this moment.

I told her
I just want to stand here face to face
and experience the intimacy
of staring into her eyes,
knowing, just knowing,
whatever happens next
can't kill the vibe before our mood subsides.

Because we've both
been in situations
that in the end meant absolutely nothing,
so I told her
that if she opened her heart, I'd open mine
and do my best to try and make it mean something.

I told her
I wanna take my time
and appreciate
the way destiny dealt this hand.
Patiently waiting,
inches away from her lips,
to catch wherever her tender kisses land,
I said,

"Maybe this isn't the right time
but the road to hell
is paved with good intentions.
I'm just trying to say we've both been through
some things, and this time
I really wanna know who I'll be kissing."

So she leaned into me,
an inch closer,
as if to close our distance.
I watched the look in her eyes
and the tilt of her neck
create a path of least resistance.

I spoke again
but she stole the moment
before I could even finish my sentence
and that little act
of passive assertion
was all it took to make our whole night
submissive.

MESMERIZED

What if I told you
you were just a thought?
A submissive
little fantasy
suppressed
within the quiet
confines of my dirty mind
that somehow got twisted
and left me feeling,
thinking,
and wondering to myself
if I could be the first man
to hold your hand
like it was the last time.

And somewhere in the awkwardness
of my heart's
wayward misdirection
I started to see
goodness in you,
no matter how deep
any imperfection lies,

so I decided to shed my skin,
attract you
with who I am within,
and put away that mask
concealing
who I was
behind that lustful disguise
for the chance
to let you know
that I'm not afraid to fall for you.

Because I'm someone
who's willing to go
through all the lows
to feel your highs,
for the chance to live
out my wish
and receive your heart
as a gift.
Because I believe I'm man enough
to be the beau
that cuts all ties
for the chance to live
on the tip of your tongue,
feel the press of your lips
and experience
the spiral of Jacob's ladder,
holding you in my arms

when we rise,
you know,
to be seen by you,
up close and personal,
to dance in your light
and be mesmerized
by all the things
that makes you so wonderful in my eyes.

ENTER THE DRAGON

Woman, you are
mysterious like that silhouette
I only find in my darkest dreams.
Erotic as porn
I've made wet,
exploding on my silver screen.

You make every dirty thought
I've had
pure enough to be clean
and leave me wondering why
all my prayers to God
border on the obscene.

Sometimes
I lie here and obsess
over the shade of your pretty eyes,
wishing I could let the cum
on my tip drip
all over your caramel mocha thighs.

I can't wait to see
all those faces you make
during that nefarious moment when
your hourglass shape
does whatever it takes
to make the strength of my erection bend.

You live in that shy blush
that leaves me so uptight,
wishing I could unwind.
You make the whole world hush
waiting for your skin
to brush up against mine.

I can feel your spoon
stir my blood
with every wicked thought I think.
I can't wait to see Eden
in the millionth of a second
it takes your eyes to blink.

You bask
in that long, hot breath.
The moment my affections peak
you come alive in your bottle,
dancing in the depths
of that penetration I seek.

You make every drop
of my ivory
feel so bittersweet.
Your saliva is drenched in a eureka
moment that can't wait
to polish me till I squeak.

Come jump the broom
and let me suck your neck
all the way down your slender back
and let me hold you
on the arch of my tongue
kissing every corner of your crack.

Come
let me wet your canvas
till my kisses burn like a tattoo
and finally appease
this fire-breathing dragon in me
that's been so hungry for you.

PAINT YOU BLACK

It took the light of every single solitary star
to make the shape of your body so heavenly
until the first Eve became a total eclipse
that made every dawn a shade of your ebony.

I stood there as He took the exact amounts
of beauty and elegance to shape your essence.
I hid my face until the summit of my shyness
became a masculinity in your presence.

I felt your body of earth and water
promise to quench my hunger and my thirst —
that is, until I saw Him spark your wildfire
and felt a fluorescent desire to put you first.

And at that moment, all of creation could feel
the wind He blew into your soul to form your spirit
until your moans became the sound of music
and all the angels in heaven could stop to hear it.

I watched the flames of countless stars burn
until each one slowly became a cinder.
I watched Him mold the clay and ash of stardust
into that brown sugar that makes you so tender.

And at that moment I struggled with my innocence
as I stood in the darkness of your jet,
wishing I could lick whatever it was
He used to make you so soft and wet.

I saw the bravest creatures come out their haven
in the darkness of your abyss
and become dark horses, panthers and ravens
in the wake of His great bliss.

They went through the eye of the great needle
He used to sew the perfection of your lining
and one by one came out the other side,
embracing your rhythm in the stitching of his timing.

I felt him engrave His likeness into you
until the base of His chisel made me tremble.
He said if His joy of creating was a sign,
your presence would always be His symbol.

And at that moment I wanted you so bad
I could feel you in my bone marrow
as He enriched you with enough melanin
to seduce Caesar and subdue a pharaoh.

I looked through the savage fire
until it became the radiance of your sheen.
He wore your halo around His finger
so I bowed down to kiss the ring.

I smiled and your true beauty was revealed
when you looked and gave it back.
I chose this struggle; my fate was sealed
when I saw Him paint you black.

THE PREY

Are you man enough
to love her at her very worst?
Remain steadfast and as faithful as an old blood oath?
Lose your ego whenever you put your wallet in her purse
and remember that a lady should always cum first?

Are you man enough
to show her loyalty like you just married into the mob?
Give her the same attention in the light as you do in the dark?
Remember what you put in her mind will always remain in her heart
and understand she's more than a woman, she's a gift from your God?

Are you man enough
to show her boldness with no fear of her rejections?
Remember the truth was made to shame all of her deceptions?
Understand she craves charisma from someone who'll shower her with affection?
Spend every waking moment in this struggle, striving towards her perfection?

Are you man enough
to think outside the box until she gets the point of your explanation?
Undress her with a raw sex appeal that's only found in your conversation?
Remember rose petals and butterflies were made to stimulate her imagination
but the character of your inner man was meant to pique all her dark temptations?

Are you man enough
to use metaphors to describe the lining of her pretty little symmetry?
Understand patience is a virtue so give her time like infinity?
Show her how you've been making room in your very soul for her entity
and tell her you need her in your life to be the divine in your divinity?

Are you man enough
to understand there will be no guarantees when you pursue this woman?
All the eyes of the world are waiting on God to give them something.
Give due diligence and fight the good fight even if it leaves you with nothing.
Sacrifice yourself and, if nothing else, become the prey she'll always be hunting.

EXODUS: DESTINY

On the lines of this blank sheet of paper,

the spirit of poetry becomes mine.

And whatever I make her,

her vast body of unwritten words

find form,

waiting for me to shape her

into anything my heart desires.

Her spark of imagination

burns

like a thousand bonfires,

lives on

long after I'm gone

and this body expires.

Measuring her degree of beauty by how much I want it,

forever sealing who I am, was and will be in this moment,

leaving no clue of why she came and the mystery behind it,

only offering immortality to the soul that ever finds it,

leading me to believe the reader will hang on my every word

like one day I'll say something

no eyes have seen or ears have heard,

something that will change hearts and minds with a new point of view

or find something within us all that we never knew.

Her ink becomes the paperweight she keeps using to attest to me.

On this sheet of paper, one man's fate

can help shape

the whole world's destiny...

www.ingramcontent.com/pod-product-compliance
Lightning Source LLC
La Vergne TN
LVHW022323080426
835508LV00041B/2233